THE CLIMATE CRISIS IN
THE SOUTHEAST

by Heather C. Morris

FOCUS
READERS®

NAVIGATOR

WWW.FOCUSREADERS.COM

Focus Readers is distributed by North Star Editions:
sales@northstareditions.com | 888-417-0195

Produced for Focus Readers by Red Line Editorial.

Content Consultant: Alessandra Jerolleman, PhD, Associate Professor of Emergency Management, Jacksonville State University

Photographs ©: Shutterstock Images, cover, 1; Paolo Nespoli/NASA, 4–5; iStockphoto, 7, 8–9, 13, 14–15, 25, 29; Red Line Editorial, 10; Raeford Brown/AP Images, 17; Jason Lee/ The Sun News/AP Images, 19; Curtis Compton/Atlanta Journal-Constitution/AP Images, 21; Steve Helber/AP Images, 22–23; Allen Creative/Steve Allen/Alamy, 27

Library of Congress Cataloging-in-Publication Data
Names: Morris, Heather C., author.
Title: The climate crisis in the Southeast / by Heather C. Morris.
Description: Lake Elmo, MN : Focus Readers, [2024] | Series: The climate
  crisis in America | Includes index. | Audience: Grades 4-6
Identifiers: LCCN 2023002954 (print) | LCCN 2023002955 (ebook) | ISBN
  9781637396353 (hardcover) | ISBN 9781637396926 (paperback) | ISBN
  9781637398005 (pdf) | ISBN 9781637397497 (ebook)
Subjects: LCSH: Endangered ecosystems--Southern States--Juvenile
  literature. | Biodiversity--Climatic factors--Southern States--Juvenile
  literature.
Classification: LCC QH76.5.S69 M67 2024 (print) | LCC QH76.5.S69 (ebook)
  | DDC 577.27--dc23/eng/20230124
LC record available at https://lccn.loc.gov/2023002954
LC ebook record available at https://lccn.loc.gov/2023002955

Printed in the United States of America
Mankato, MN
082023

ABOUT THE AUTHOR

Heather C. Morris is a research scientist and author with more than 15 years' experience supporting NASA science projects. She is currently working on a global climate-monitoring project. When she's not in the lab, she enjoys writing fiction and nonfiction books for kids who love science and imagination.

TABLE OF CONTENTS

CHAPTER 1

HURRICANE IRMA

In September 2017, a storm began swirling. Warm ocean water made it larger and stronger. Scientists used satellites to track the storm. They warned people nearby to get ready to leave the area. Many people stored supplies. Or they packed suitcases. Others were not able or could not afford to leave.

The International Space Station captured a photo of Hurricane Irma on September 5, 2017.

When the storm finally hit the coast of Florida, it was named Hurricane Irma.

The hurricane tore roofs off buildings. It pulled up trees and flooded houses. It left people without electricity. Scientists said Irma was one of the strongest hurricanes ever. After it passed, houses were smashed. Bridges were broken. Slowly, people who could began cleaning up. Repairing the damage cost billions of dollars. And it took years to finish.

In the Southeast, more dangerous storms are one effect of **climate change**. Climate is the normal weather for an area over a long period of time. Weather can change from day to day. Climate changes

This home in Florida was knocked off its foundation and destroyed after Irma.

slowly, over many years. The changes are so slow that people may not notice. But climates are changing so fast that scientists are worried. These changes are hurting people, plants, and animals. They are making it very difficult for people to live in some places.

CHAPTER 2

FROM BEACHES TO MOUNTAINS

The Southeast includes Virginia, North Carolina, South Carolina, Georgia, Alabama, and Florida. These states all share a common climate. This climate is partly due to latitude. Latitude is how far north or south a place is from the **equator**. Areas near the equator are tropical. A tropical climate is hot, humid,

The Everglades are in southern Florida. The area is home to a huge variety of plants and animals.

and rainy. These conditions last all year. The southern tip of Florida is tropical. However, most of the Southeast is subtropical. It is a bit farther north.

THE SOUTHEAST

Summers tend to be hot. Winters are often mild. North Carolina and Virginia are farther north. Their winters are colder.

The Southeast also tends to be humid. That's because of warm ocean waters. Each state touches the Atlantic Ocean or the Gulf of Mexico. Warm, wet air blows in from the sea. It mixes with dry, cold air from the west. The mix often produces rain and strong storms. Powerful thunderstorms are common all year. In summer and fall, hurricanes become a threat, too. They can cause a variety of damage, including flooding.

Coastal and river areas are especially at risk of flooding. The Southeast features several river systems. Strong storms can cause these bodies of water to overflow.

Ocean waters also create differences in the region's climate. Water takes longer to heat and cool than land does.

THE LUMBEE PEOPLE

Wetlands are common in the Southeast. People in the region have long depended on these areas. The Lumbee people have lived along the Lumbee River for thousands of years. This river flows slowly among swamps in North Carolina. For many years, the swampy lands protected the Lumbee from white settlers. These settlers later took land from all the **Indigenous** groups. Some Indigenous groups even moved to the swamps for safety. Today, the Lumbee Tribe is the largest tribe on the East Coast.

Alabama's coast experiences much milder temperatures than areas farther from shore.

So, the coasts have milder temperatures. In contrast, places inland face wider temperature swings.

Elevation affects the climate as well. Elevation is how high the land is compared with sea level. The Appalachian Mountains lie along the western part of the region. These areas are cooler because of their higher elevation. They also can receive snowfall.

CHAPTER 3

CRISES IN THE SOUTHEAST

The climate crisis is already changing the Southeast. For example, average temperatures are rising. Temperatures at night have risen more than daytime temperatures. And temperatures are still rising.

Warmer nights mean plants cannot cool off. Plus, higher temperatures also

Extreme heat tends to be more intense in cities. Atlanta, Georgia, is at high risk.

increase **evaporation**. Dry periods can become even drier. These changes make some crops harder to grow. Fewer crops mean less food. Farmers cannot make as much money. Farm animals are affected, too. These animals struggle to cool off.

THE ACF RIVER BASIN

Three major rivers flow through Georgia, Alabama, and Florida. They are the Apalachicola, the Chattahoochee, and the Flint. Together, they form the ACF basin. These rivers provide water to cities and farms. But from 2011 to 2012, Georgia suffered a drought. Water in the ACF basin ran low. Crops worth millions of dollars withered. Wells ran dry. State leaders are working to protect and share this important resource.

This home on the North Carolina shore is an example of how erosion threatens buildings on the Southeast coast.

Higher temperatures lead to other changes, too. Many glaciers are melting. Warmer water also takes up more space than cooler water. These changes are raising sea levels. Rising sea levels are already causing problems on the Southeast coast. They are wearing away shores. This process is called erosion.

Sea level rise also is making coastal floods more intense and more common. Some flooding comes from rising high tides. Rising sea levels are increasing these types of floods. Storms can also cause flooding. They bring rain and storm surges. That's when storms raise sea levels. The ocean water crashes onto the shore. With higher sea levels, storm surges reach farther inland and cause much more damage.

Plus, climate change is making storms stronger and more common. The added rainfall combines with rising sea levels. Heavier rainfall also increases flooding near rivers. Many rivers are near cities.

In 2020, heavy rain overflowed the Waccamaw River. That caused floods in Socastee, South Carolina.

As a result, river floods are affecting more and more people. Flooding is becoming an extreme threat across the Southeast.

LEARNING FROM HURRICANES

In 2016, middle school students in St. Marys, Georgia, watched Hurricane Matthew closely. The storm swept up the Atlantic coast. It barely missed their homes. But the winds and high water still flooded their town. However, the kids saw more than just a problem. They also saw an opportunity.

With the help of adults and teachers, the students measured the land around their school. They mapped places that were lower than others. Next, they collected standing water to test for diseases. They gathered all this information. They used it to help others prepare for the next storm.

Adults paid attention to the students. Now, homes and businesses are built differently.

A storm surge from Hurricane Matthew floods St. Marys, Georgia, in October 2016.

Because of the students' hard work, St. Marys is more prepared for severe storms and a changing climate.

CHAPTER 4

HOW TO HELP

Burning **fossil fuels** is the major cause of the climate crisis. Fossil fuels include oil, natural gas, and coal. Burning them makes energy. But it also releases **greenhouse gases** into the atmosphere. The gases trap heat and lead to climate change. To slow climate change, people must burn much less fossil fuel.

In 2021, 57 percent of Virginia's electricity came from natural gas.

The Southeast can shift to new energy sources. One example is solar power. Solar panels use sunlight to make electricity. They release far less greenhouse gases than fossil fuels. So, solar power can replace coal and gas power plants.

Even so, people still need to adapt to the climate crisis. One problem is dealing with rising temperatures. Extreme heat can make people sick. Cities are taking steps to solve this issue. Some are installing cool roofs. These roofs reflect heat. That helps lower a building's temperature. Cities are planting more trees, too. Shade helps areas stay cool.

Out of all states, North Carolina produced the fourth-most solar power in 2022. Florida came in third.

Coastal communities are adapting to rising sea levels. Some cities are building homes and businesses farther from water. Others are building higher up. Savannah, Georgia, installed sensors to track sea levels. The sensors help the city predict future problems. Other cities are installing living shorelines. Living shorelines include plants and oyster reefs. They help prevent erosion.

Some cities are reducing flooding from storms. One method uses rain gardens. Workers dig ditches in the ground. Rain flows into the ditches and through plants inside them. The plants help slow and trap water. Walls block pollution. But they let water through. This clean water flows into the sewers.

Farms also need to adapt to climate change. Scientists are developing hardier crops. These crops can handle more rain and higher temperatures.

People are also protecting **ecosystems**. For example, forests are a key part of the Southeast. They provide shelter for animals. They remove greenhouse gases

River cane is important to the Cherokee. People are restoring the native plant to the Southeast.

from the air. They also supply materials for paper and lumber.

The Eastern Band of Cherokee Indians live in North Carolina in the Great Smoky Mountains. These Cherokee people are studying native plants there. Together, the Cherokee and forest rangers are protecting these plant species. This work helps restore the forest's **biodiversity**. That can help it survive climate change.

Everyone can help fight the climate crisis. Young people can learn about the climate risks in their region. They can also attend climate protests. These actions bring attention to important

LONGLEAF PINES

Longleaf pine trees once grew all over the Southeast. But not many are left. Today, people are planting more of them. The pines grow in wet or dry soil. They can handle severe storms. More longleaf pines will restore forests. They will also help those forests survive a changing climate.

Young people can explain why communities should help those who can't afford to adapt to climate change.

issues. Young people can also talk with their families. They can talk with leaders in their schools and communities. They can explain why climate action matters. Young people can also communicate with lawmakers. They can demand that lawmakers act on climate.

FOCUS ON
THE SOUTHEAST

Write your answers on a separate piece of paper.

1. Write a few sentences describing the typical climate in the Southeast.

2. What do you think are the worst threats the Southeast faces from climate change? Why?

3. Which areas are most at risk of flooding?

   A. coastal areas
   B. inland areas
   C. mountain areas

4. Most of the Southeast is within what latitude?

   A. arctic
   B. subtropical
   C. tropical

Answer key on page 32.

GLOSSARY

biodiversity
The number of different species that live in an area.

climate change
A human-caused global crisis involving long-term changes in Earth's temperature and weather patterns.

ecosystems
Communities of living things and how they interact with their surrounding environments.

equator
An imaginary line that runs around the middle of Earth.

evaporation
When liquid water turns to water vapor.

fossil fuels
Energy sources that come from the remains of plants and animals that died long ago.

greenhouse gases
Gases that trap heat in Earth's atmosphere, causing climate change.

Indigenous
Native to a region, or belonging to ancestors who lived in a region before colonists arrived.

TO LEARN MORE

BOOKS

Conca, Carol. *Florida*. Minneapolis: Abdo Publishing, 2023.

Henzel, Cynthia Kennedy. *Redesigning Cities to Fight Climate Change*. Lake Elmo, MN: Focus Readers, 2023.

Raij, Emily. *Climate Change and You: How Climate Change Affects Your Life*. North Mankato, MN: Capstone Press, 2020.

NOTE TO EDUCATORS

Visit **www.focusreaders.com** to find lesson plans, activities, links, and other resources related to this title.

INDEX

Answer Key: 1. Answers will vary; **2.** Answers will vary; **3.** A; **4.** B